The OWL and The PUSSY-CAT

WELCOME TO
Professor
COMFORT'S
*Story & Music
Hour*

ASSISTED BY

ARABELLA

*for
Michael
Patrick
Hearn*

The OWL and The

based on the poem by

Edward Lear

HILARY KNIGHT'S
PUSSY-CAT

Macmillan Publishing Company
New York

Macmillan Publishing Company,
a division of Macmillan, Inc.
866 Third Avenue, New York, N.Y. 10022
Collier Macmillan Canada, Inc.
Printed in the United States of America
10 9 8 7 6 5 4 3 2 1
Library of Congress Cataloging in Publication Data
Knight, Hilary.
Hilary Knight's The owl and the pussy-cat.
Summary: Captivated by Edward Lear's poem, a boy and
girl turn into the owl and the pussycat and set sail in
a pea green boat for The Land Where the Bong Tree Grows.
1. Children's poetry, English. [1. Nonsense verses.
2. English poetry] I. Lear, Edward, 1812–1888. Owl and
the pussy-cat. II. Title. III. Title: Owl and the pussy-cat.
PR4879.L2O9   1983b   821'.914   83-9844
ISBN 0-02-750900-1

'Arabella! warm up the muffins and cocoa.

.... *I have the perfect story for you!*

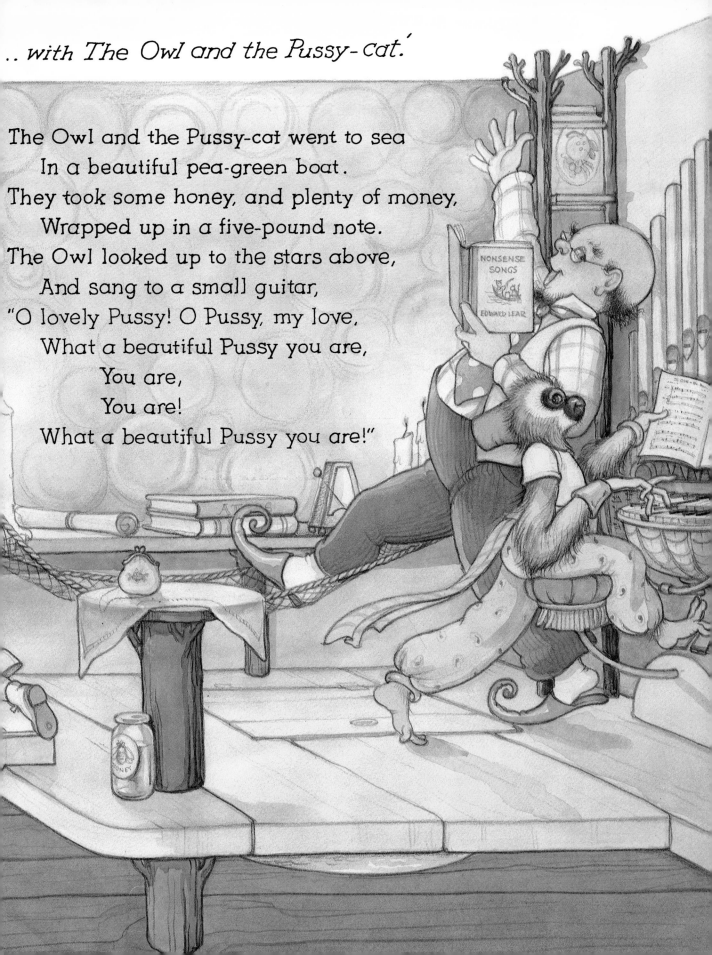

The Owl and the Pussy-cat went to sea
    In a beautiful pea-green boat.
They took some honey, and plenty of money,
    Wrapped up in a five-pound note.
The Owl looked up to the stars above,
    And sang to a small guitar,
"O lovely Pussy! O Pussy, my love,
    What a beautiful Pussy you are,
        You are,
        You are!
What a beautiful Pussy you are!"

Pussy said to the Owl, "You elegant fowl!
    How charmingly sweet you sing!
O let us be married! too long we have tarried:
    But what shall we do for a ring?"
They sailed away, for a year and a day,
    To the land where the Bong-tree grows
And there in a wood a Piggy-wig stood
    With a ring at the end of his nose,
        His nose,
        His nose,
    With a ring at the end of his nose.

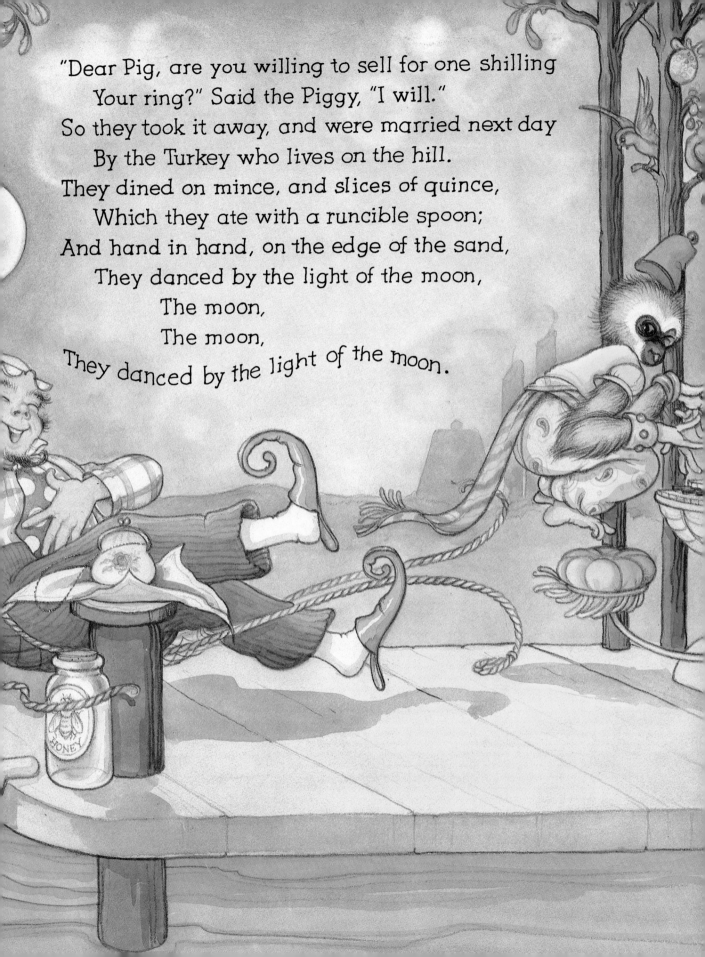

"Dear Pig, are you willing to sell for one shilling
    Your ring?" Said the Piggy, "I will."
So they took it away, and were married next day
    By the Turkey who lives on the hill.
They dined on mince, and slices of quince,
    Which they ate with a runcible spoon;
And hand in hand, on the edge of the sand,
    They danced by the light of the moon,
        The moon,
        The moon,
They danced by the light of the moon.

'All together now!'

The Owl and the Pussy-cat went to sea
in a beautiful pea-green boat.
They took some honey, and plenty of money
wrapped up in a five pound note.

Said the Piggy, 'I will.'

So they took it away, and were
married next day by the Turkey

who lives on the hill.

They dined on mince,
and slices of quince,
which they ate with
a runcible spoon;

They danced
by the light
of the
moon.

.
good
night
.

0049-84